ACCA
Performance Management (PM)

First edition 2007, Thirteenth edition January 2019

ISBN 9781 5097 2393 5

e ISBN 9781 5097 2420 8

British Library Cataloguing-in-Publication Data

A catalogue record for this book is available from the British Library

Published by

BPP Learning Media Ltd,
BPP House, Aldine Place,
142-144 Uxbridge Road,
London W12 8AA

www.bpp.com/learningmedia

Printed in the UK

Your learning materials, published by BPP Learning Media Ltd, are printed on paper obtained from traceable sustainable sources.

Welcome to BPP Learning Media's ACCA **Passcards** for **Performance Management (PM)**.

- They **focus on your exam** and **save you time**.

- They incorporate **diagrams** to kick start your memory.

- They follow the overall **structure** of the BPP Study Texts, but BPP's ACCA **Passcards** are not just a condensed book. Each card has been separately designed for clear presentation. Topics are self contained and can be grasped visually.

- ACCA **Passcards** are still **just the right size** for pockets, briefcases and bags.

Run through the **Passcards** as often as you can during your final revision period. The day before the exam, try to go through the **Passcards** again! You will then be well on your way to passing your exams.

Good luck!

For reference to the Bibliography of the Performance Management Passcards please go to:
learningmedia.bpp.com and visit the "Student" section.

1: Managing information

Topic List

The role of information systems

Communication of information

Controls and security

Internal sources of information

External sources of information

Information systems and technology are becoming increasingly important for businesses. The topics covered in this chapter and the next chapter could be tested in objective test questions or as part of a Section C constructed response question.

The role of information systems

Organisations require information for:

- Planning: available resources, possible time scales and likely outcomes
- Controlling: to assess whether activities are proceeding as planned and to take corrective action if required
- Recording transactions
- Performance measurement: comparisons against budget or plan
- Decision making

Information system costs include:

- Hardware and software costs
- Implementation costs (eg labour and training)
- Day to day costs

Networks

Are groups of machines that are connected together, allowing information and resources to be shared.

Intranets

Are mini versions of the internet, held on servers that an organisation's members can access. They contain a variety of information of importance to the staff.

Extranets

Are a form of internet that authorised outsiders to the organisation can access using a username and password. They are a useful means for business partners to share information.

Wireless technology

Allows communication using electromagnetic, radio and microwave signals.

Benefits include remote working and increased mobility, often increased productivity and reduced costs.

Controls required over the generation of internal information

→ **In routine reports**
eg consistent format to ensure accuracy

→ **In ad-hoc reports**
eg ensure information does not already exist in another format

→ **Over distributing internal information**
eg procedures manuals

→ **Over information held on servers**
eg passwords

→ **Other controls**
eg email policy

Procedures to ensure the security of highly confidential information that is not for external consumption

- Logical access systems
- Database controls
  - Inference controls
  - Passwords
- Personnel security planning
- Firewalls
- Encryption
- Authentication
- Dial back security

Costs

of the collection, processing and production of internal data

▶ **Direct data capture costs**
eg use of bar-coding

▶ **Processing costs**
eg inputting data to the MIS

▶ **Cost of inefficient use of information**
eg information disseminated more widely than needed

Principal internal sources of management accounting information

- Financial accounting records
- Systems of control over transactions (eg inventory control systems)
- Payroll, production records, timesheets
- Staff (collected formally or informally)

In today's competitive market, where the pace of change in information systems and technology is rapid, organisations must be flexible enough to adapt to change quickly and must plan for expansion, growth and innovation within information systems.

External information is used to different degrees depending on the level and type of decision.

INTERNAL

EXTERNAL

Operational   Tactical   Strategic

External information can contribute to planning (eg market research informing sales budgets), decision-making (eg through competitor research) and control (eg from benchmarking).

Common external sources of information

- Business directories
- Associations
- Government agencies
- Consumer panels
- Customers
- Suppliers
- Internet
- Databases
- Market research
- Data warehouses (internal + external sources)

External information is used in the management accounting system depending on its quality. **Quantitative** data is easier to use. **Benchmarking** uses external information to help set targets.

Costs associated with external sources

Direct search costs
eg subscriptions to magazines

Indirect access costs
eg spurious accuracy

Management costs
eg wasted time on excessive processing

Infrastructure costs
eg maintenance of computer server

Time theft
eg information overload

Disadvantages
■ May not be entirely relevant
■ Bias
■ Accuracy should be questioned
■ May not be available in correct form
■ Can be expensive

Note that the costs of market research can be considerable and that the internet can significantly reduce search time and search costs.

Advantages
■ Save time and money as secondary data is cheaper than primary

Notes

2: Information systems and data analytics

Performance management information systems provide the information that enables performance measurement to take place.

Such systems include transaction processing systems (TPS), management information systems (MIS), executive information systems (EIS) and enterprise resource planning systems (ERP).

Customer relationship management (CRM) systems help to better understand the customer in the hope of generating customer loyalty.

The three Vs of Big Data are volume, velocity and variety.

Management accounting information
can be used to support strategic planning, control and decision-making.

Strategic management accounting differs from traditional management accounting because it has an **external** orientation and a **future** orientation.

Examples of strategic management accounting

- Analysis of competitors' costs
- Product profitability
- Customer profitability
- Pricing decisions
- Cost/benefits of capacity expansion
- Analysis of decisions to enter (or leave) a business area
- Brand values
- Shareholder wealth
- Impact of acquisitions and mergers
- Analysis of competitors' potential reactions to a strategy

Management control

The process by which managers ensure that resources are obtained and used effectively and efficiently in the accomplishment of the organisation's objectives. It is sometimes called **tactics** or **tactical planning.**

Management control decisions need to support an organisation's strategic plans.

Characteristics of management control

- Short-term and non-strategic
- Management control planning activities include preparing annual sales budget
- Management control activities include ensuring budget targets are (at least) reached
- Carried out in a series of routine and regular planning and comparison procedures
- Management control information covers the whole organisation, is routinely collected/ disseminated, is often quantitative and commonly expressed in money terms
  - Cash flow forecasts
  - Variance analysis reports
  - Staffing levels
- Source of information likely to be **endogenous** (from within the organisation)

Management control and strategic planning compared

Example

The decision to launch a new brand of frozen foods is a strategic plan, but the choice of ingredients for the meals is a management control decision.

Conflict

Long-term strategic plans can conflict with the shorter-term objectives of management control:

- Performance measures/control measures do not take strategic direction into account.
- Strategic imperatives might not be properly communicated to middle management.
- Strategic planning information might be difficult to measure.

Operational control/planning

The process of ensuring that specific tasks are carried out effectively and efficiently.

Management control v operational control

Operational control decisions are more narrowly focused, carried out within a shorter time frame and taken by managers less senior in the organisation.

Operational control focuses on individual tasks whereas management control is concerned with the sum of all tasks. (Anthony, 1965)

Example

Strategic plan

Senior management decide sales should increase by 5% pa for at least five years.

Management control decision

Sales quotas are assigned to each sales territory.

Operational control decision

Managers of sales territories specify weekly targets for each sales representative.

Characteristics

- Short-term and non-strategic
- Occurs in **all aspects** of an organisation's activities and needed for day-to-day implementation of plans
- Often carried out at short notice
- Information likely to have an **endogenous** source, to be detailed transaction data, quantitative and expressed in terms of units/hours
- Includes customer orders and cash receipts

Good information

- Relevant
- Complete
- Accurate
- Clear
- Usable with confidence
- Appropriately communicated (to the right person using the correct method)
- Manageable volume
- Timely
- Cost effective

What management accounting information helps managers to do (its objectives)

- Measure performance
- Control the business
- Plan for the future
- Make decisions

Management accounting information is used for **score keeping, problem solving** and **attention directing.**

Features that characterise management accounting information in particular

- Forward looking
- Neutral (free from bias)
- Financial, non-financial, quantitative or qualitative

Information requirements vary significantly across different types of organisational structure (eg functional basis vs network organisation).

Transaction processing systems (TPS)

Transaction processing systems collect, store, modify and retrieve the transactions of an organisation.

Key characteristics
■ Controlled processing
■ Inflexibility
■ Rapid response
■ Reliability

Management information systems (MIS)

Management information systems generate information for monitoring performance (eg productivity information) and maintaining co-ordination (eg between purchasing and accounts payable).

Executive information systems (EIS)

Executive information systems provide a generalised computing and communication environment to senior managers to support strategic decisions.

Key characteristics

- Report on existing operations
- Little analytical capability
- Relatively inflexible
- Internally focused

Key characteristics

- Menu driven user friendly interfaces
- Interactive graphics
- Communication capabilities linking the executive to external databases

Enterprise resource planning systems (ERP)

Enterprise resource planning systems are software systems designed to support and automate the business processes of medium-sized and large organisations. They aid the flow of information between functions within an organisation and can manage connections to outside suppliers.

All departments that are involved in operations or production are integrated in one system.

Key characteristics

- Work in real-time
- Multiple languages and currencies
- Integrate the key processes in an organisation
- Decision support features
- Extranet links to major suppliers and customers

Customer relationship management (CRM) systems

CRM systems are software applications that specialise in providing information concerning an organisation's products, services and customers.

Big Data refers to the mass of data that society creates each year.

3 Vs

Volume

Very large volumes of data captured. Eg via embedded sensors in everyday items.

Velocity

Data produced at very high speeds.

Timeliness is critical to usefulness.

Variety

Consists of structured and unstructured data.

Structured

= traditional data sets

Unstructured

= majority of data created by social media

Benefits to organisations undertaking Big Data analytics

Benefits	Comment
Examine vast quantities of data relatively quickly	Big Data analytics allows for large quantities of data to be examined to identify trends and correlations eg shopper buying habits.
Improves organisational decision making	Better data analysis helps management to take advantage of current social trends by introducing new products to meet customers' needs.
Greater focus on the individual customer	Organisations can target special offers or discounts directly to individual customers to entice repeat business.
Cost reduction	Improved data about customers and internal operations may help to reduce costs. This is illustrated in the following case study.

Notes

3: Costing

Topic List

Costing

Absorption costing

Absorption costing vs marginal costing

You will have covered the basics of these costing methods in your earlier studies but you need to make sure you are familiar with the concepts and techniques so you can answer interpretation questions.

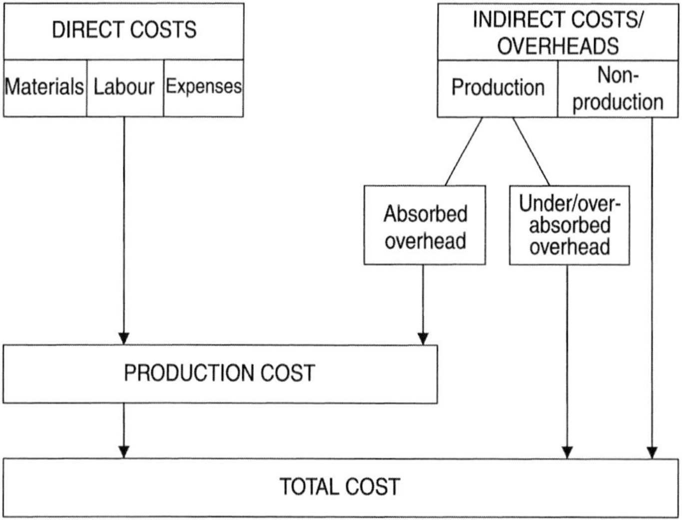

DIRECT COSTS		
Materials	Labour	Expenses

INDIRECT COSTS/ OVERHEADS	
Production	Non-production

Absorbed overhead

Under/over-absorbed overhead

PRODUCTION COST

TOTAL COST

Cost accounting

A management information system which analyses past, present and future data to provide a bank of data for the management accountant to use.

Costing

The process of determining the cost of products, services or activities. Methods include absorption costing and process costing.

What is absorption costing?

Absorption costing is a method of sharing out overheads incurred amongst units produced.

1 Allocation

2 Apportionment

3 Absorption ———▶ under/over-absorbed overhead

Practical reasons for using absorption costing

- Inventory valuations
- Pricing decisions
- Establishing profitability of products

Arguments in favour of absorption costing

- When sales fluctuate because of seasonality in sales demand but production is held constant, absorption costing avoids large fluctuations in profit.

- Marginal costing fails to recognise the importance of working to full capacity and its effects on pricing decisions if cost plus method of pricing is used.

- Prices based on marginal cost (minimum prices) do not guarantee that contribution will cover fixed costs.

- In the long run all costs are variable, and absorption costing recognises these long-run variable costs.

- It is consistent with the requirements of accounting standards.

Arguments in favour of marginal costing

- It shows how an organisation's cash flows and profits are affected by changes in sales volumes since contribution varies in direct proportion to units sold.

- By using absorption costing and setting a production level greater than sales demand, profits can be manipulated.

- Separating fixed and variable costs is vital for decision-making.

- For short-run decisions in which fixed costs do not change (such as short-run tactical decisions seeking to make the best use of existing resources), the decision rule is to choose the alternative which maximises **contribution**, fixed costs being irrelevant.

4: Modern management accounting techniques

Topic List

Activity based costing (ABC)

Target costing

Life cycle costing

Throughput accounting

Environmental accounting

All five techniques covered are equally important and equally examinable. You need to develop a broad background in management accounting techniques.

These topics could feature in Section A or B of the exam.

Features of a modern manufacturing environment

- An increase in support services, which are unaffected by changes in production volume, varying instead with the range and complexity of products
- An increase in overheads as a proportion of total costs

Inadequacies of absorption costing

- Implies all overheads are related to production volume
- Developed at a time when organisations produced only a narrow range of products and overheads were only a small fraction of total costs
- Tends to allocate too great a proportion of overheads to higher volume products
- Can sometimes lead to over production

Outline of an ABC system

1 Identify major activities.

2 Use cost allocation and apportionment methods to these activities (**cost pools**).

3 Identify the **cost drivers** which determine the size of the costs of each activity.

4 For each activity, calculate an absorption rate per unit of cost driver.

5 Charge overhead costs to products on the basis of their usage of the activity (the number of cost drivers they use).

Cost drivers

- Volume related (eg labour hours) for costs that vary with production volume in the short-term (eg power costs)
- Transactions in support departments for other costs (eg number of production runs for the cost of setting-up production runs)

Example

Cost of goods inwards department = \$10,000

Cost driver for goods inwards activity = number of deliveries

During 20X0 there were 1,000 deliveries, 200 of which related to product X. 4,000 units of product X were produced.

Cost per unit of cost driver = \$10,000 ÷ 1,000 = \$10

Cost of activity attributable to product X = \$10 × 200 = \$2,000

Cost of activity per unit of X = \$2,000 ÷ 4,000 = \$0.50

Merits of ABC

☑ Simple (once information obtained)

☑ Focuses attention on what causes costs to increase (cost drivers)

☑ Absorption rates more closely linked to causes of overheads because many cost drivers are used

Criticisms of ABC

☒ More complex and so should only be introduced if provides additional information

☒ Can one cost driver explain the behaviour of all items in a cost pool?

☒ Cost drivers might be difficult to identify

4: Modern management accounting techniques

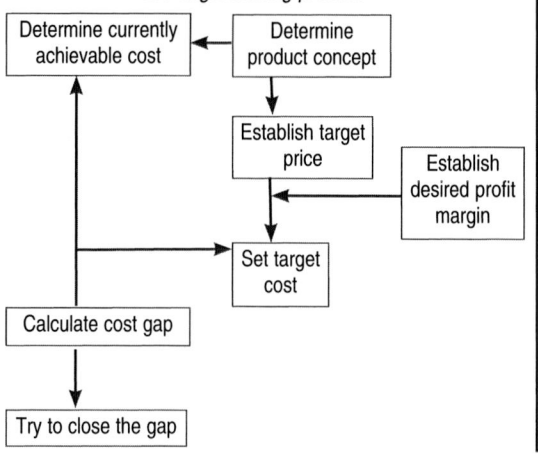

The target costing process

- Determine currently achievable cost
- Determine product concept
- Establish target price
- Establish desired profit margin
- Set target cost
- Calculate cost gap
- Try to close the gap

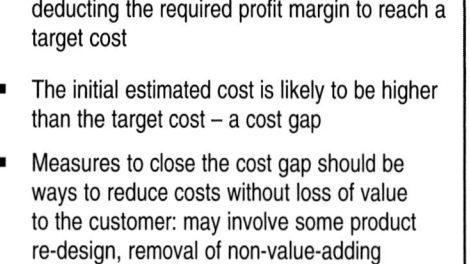

Target costing

- Involves setting a target cost by first of all identifying a target selling price and then deducting the required profit margin to reach a target cost

- The initial estimated cost is likely to be higher than the target cost – a cost gap

- Measures to close the cost gap should be ways to reduce costs without loss of value to the customer: may involve some product re-design, removal of non-value-adding features, use of more standard components, alternative materials for some product parts

| Activity based costing (ABC) | Target costing | **Life cycle costing** | Throughput accounting | Environmental accounting |

Life cycle costing

This method tracks and accumulates costs and revenues over a product's entire life.

1. Development
2. Introduction
3. Growth
4. Maturity
5. Decline

Aim

- To obtain a satisfactory return from a product over its expected life. Life cycle costing is a planning technique rather than a traditional method of measuring and accounting for product costs.

Life cycle costs include:

- Costs incurred at product design, development and testing stage
- Advertising and sales promotion costs when the product is first introduced to the market
- Expected costs of disposal/clean-up/shutdown when the product reaches the end of its life

Advantages	**Maximising the return over the product life cycle**
■ Cost visibility is increased	■ Design costs out of products
■ Individual product profitability is better understood	■ Minimise the time to market
■ More accurate feedback information is provided on success or failure of new products	■ Minimise breakeven time
■ Useful planning technique, to forecast profitability of a new product over its life; can help to determine target sales prices and costs	■ Maximise the length of the life span
	■ Minimise product proliferation
	■ Manage the product's cashflows

Theory of constraints (TOC)

An approach to production management which aims to turn materials into sales as quickly as possible, thereby maximising the net cash generated from sales. It focuses on removing **bottlenecks** (binding constraints) to ensure evenness of production flow. (Goldratt and Cox, 1992)

Principal concepts of throughput accounting

- In the short run, all costs except materials are fixed
- The ideal inventory level is zero and so unavoidable, idle capacity in some operations must be accepted
- WIP is valued at material cost only, as no value is added and no profit earned until a sale takes place

Production concepts

1. Just-in-Time purchasing and production as much as possible
2. Use bottleneck resource to the full and as profitably as possible
3. Allow idle time on non-bottleneck resources
4. Seek to increase availability of bottleneck resource
5. When constraint on bottleneck resource is lifted and it is no longer a bottleneck, a different bottleneck resource takes over

Throughput accounting (TA)

Developed from TOC as an alternative cost and management accounting system in a Just-in-Time (JIT) production environment.

TA measurements

Throughput = Sales − Direct materials cost

Factory costs = All costs other than direct materials costs

All factory costs per period are assumed to be fixed costs.

Throughput − Factory costs = Profit

Maximising throughput and profit

Profit maximised by maximising throughput per unit of bottleneck resource (= 'factory hour').

Products can be ranked in order of profitability according to either throughput per factory hour or TA ratio (TPAR).

Throughput accounting ratio (TPAR)

$$TPAR = \frac{\text{Throughput per factory hour}}{\text{Factory cost per factory hour}}$$

A product is not profitable if its TPAR is less than 1.

Environmental management accounting (EMA)

The generation and analysis of both financial and non-financial information in order to support environmental management processes.

Typical environmental costs

- Consumables and raw materials
- Transport and travel
- Waste and effluent disposal
- Water consumption
- Energy

Why environmental costs are important

- Identifying environmental costs associated with individual products and services can assist with pricing decisions
- Ensuring compliance with regulatory standards
- Potential for cost savings

Input/output analysis

Operates on the principal that what comes in must go out. Output is split across sold and stored goods and residual (waste). Measuring these categories in physical quantities and monetary terms forces businesses to focus on environmental costs.

Flow cost accounting

Material flows through an organisation are divided into three categories

- Material
- System
- Delivery and disposal

The values and costs of each material flow are calculated. This method focuses on reducing material, thus reducing costs and having a positive effect on the environment.

Waste (negative products) are given a cost as well as good output (positive products). Seek to reduce costs of negative products.

Environmental activity-based costing

Environment related costs such as costs relating to a sewage plant or an incinerator are attributed to joint environmental cost centres.

Environment driven costs such as increased depreciation or higher staff wages are allocated to general overheads.

Life-cycle costing

Environmental costs are considered from the design stage right up to end of life costs such as decommissioning and removal.

This may influence the design of the product itself, saving on future costs.

5: Cost volume profit (CVP) analysis

Topic List

Breakeven point

C/S ratio

Sales/product mix decisions

Target profit and margin of safety

Multi-product breakeven charts

Further aspects of CVP analysis

You need to be completely confident of the aspects of breakeven analysis covered in your earlier studies.

*It is vital to remember that for multi-product breakeven analysis, a **constant product sales mix** (whenever x units of product A are sold, y units of product B and z units of product C are also sold) must be **assumed**.*

Example (J Co)

Used throughout this chapter

Budget

Product	Sales Price	Vble cost	Sales units
M	$7	$3	6,000
N	$15	$5	2,000

Fixed costs $33,000

Calculating multi-product breakeven point

- Calculate weighted average contribution per unit (from budget) = WAC per unit
- Breakeven in units = Fixed costs/WAC per unit
- Breakeven units for each product in same proportion to unit sales in the budget

Example

Budgeted cont'n = ($4 × 6,000) + ($10 × 2,000) = $44,000

WAC per unit = $44,000/(6,000 + 2,000) = $5.50

Breakeven in total units = $33,000/$5.50 = 6,000 units

Sales of M = 6,000 × (6,000/8,000) = 4,500 units

Sales of N = 6,000 × (2,000/8,000) = 1,500 units

Calculating breakeven with multi-product C/S ratio

- Calculate budgeted contribution

- Calculate budgeted sales ratio

- Calculate weighted average C/S ratio from these two figures

- Breakeven in sales revenue = Fixed costs/Weighted average C/S ratio

- Breakeven for each product is in the same proportion to their budgeted sales revenue

Example

Budgeted contribution = ($4 × 6,000) + ($10 × 2,000) = $44,000

Budgeted sales = ($7 × 6,000) + ($15 × 2,000) = $42,000 + $30,000 = $72,000

Weighted average C/S ratio = 44,000/72,000 = 0.6111 or 61.11%

Breakeven = $33,000/0.6111 = $54,000 in sales revenue

Breakeven product M = $54,000 × (42,000/72,000) = $31,500 in sales revenue

Breakeven product N = $54,000 × (30,000/72,000) = $22,500 in sales revenue

You may be given the C/S ratio for each product in the sales mix and the budgeted proportions of sales revenue from each product.

Example

Product X C/S ratio = 33%

Product Y C/S ratio = 57%

The products will be sold in a ratio where Product X provides twice as much sales revenue as Product Y.

Selling ratio = 2:1

Weighted average C/S ratio = $(33\% \times 2/3) + (57\% \times 1/3) = 41\%$

Breakeven in sales revenue = Fixed costs/41%

Any change of products in the budgeted sales mix will alter the weighted average contribution per unit and the weighted average C/S ratio, and this will change the breakeven point.

Changing the product mix

ABC Co sells products Alpha and Beta in the ratio 5:1 at the same selling price per unit. Beta has a C/S ratio of 66.67% and the overall C/S ratio is 58.72%. How do we calculate the overall C/S ratio if the mix is changed to 2:5?

1 Calculate the missing C/S ratio

- Calculate original market share (Alpha 5/6, Beta 1/6).
- Calculate weighted C/S ratios.
  Beta: $0.6667 \times 0.1667 = 0.1111$
  Alpha: $0.5872 - 0.1111 = 0.4761$
- Calculate the missing C/S ratio.

	Alpha	Beta	Total
C/S ratio	0.5713 *	0.6667	
Market share	× 0.8333	× 0.1667	
	0.4761	0.1111	0.5872

* 0.4761/0.8333

2 Calculate the revised overall C/S ratio

	Alpha	Beta	Total
C/S ratio (as in 1)	0.5713	0.6667	
Market share (2/7:5/7)	× 0.2857	× 0.7143	
	0.1632	0.4762	0.6394

The overall C/S ratio has increased because of the increase in the proportion of the mix of the Beta, which has the higher C/S ratio.

Calculating sales to achieve target profit with multi-product sales

- Calculate weighted average contribution per unit (from budget) = WAC per unit

- Calculate target contribution = Fixed costs + Target profit

- Sales to achieve target profit = Target contribution/WAC per unit

- Units of sale for each product in same proportion to unit sales in the budget

Example continued (J Co)

The company wants to achieve target profit of $22,000.

Weighted average contribution per unit (calculated previously) = $5.50

Target contribution = $33,000 fixed costs + $22,000 target profit = $55,000

Sales to achieve target profit = $55,000/$5.50 = 10,000 units

Required sales of M = 10,000 × (6,000/8,000) = 7,500 units

Required sales of N = 10,000 × (2,000/8,000) = 2,500 units

This target is above the budgeted sales volumes.

C/S ratio method: Calculating sales to achieve target profit with multi-product sales

Sales revenue to achieve a target profit =

Target contribution/Weighted average C/S ratio

Margin of safety

A measure of risk in the budget, indicating possibility of failing to break even

Margin of safety in units = Budgeted sales – Breakeven sales

MOS expressed as a percentage of the budgeted sales

Example continued (J Co)

The company wants to achieve target profit of $22,000

Weighted average C/S ratio (calculated previously) = 0.6111

Target contribution = $55,000

Sales revenue to achieve target profit = $55,000/0.6111 = $90,000

Required sales of M = $90,000 × (42,000/72,000) = $52,500

Required sales of N = $90,000 × (30,000/72,000) = $37,500

Example continued (J Co)

From the budget

Budgeted sales in units = 8,000 units in total

Breakeven sales volume (calculated previously) = 6,000 units

Margin of safety = 2,000 units

Margin of safety = (2,000/8,000) × 100% = 25%

Actual sales can fall short of the budget by 25% (in the budgeted proportions in the sales mix) before the company fails to break even

Breakeven chart

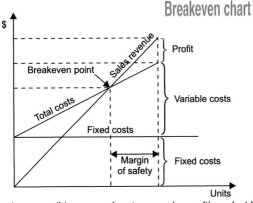

A multi-product breakeven chart can only be drawn on the assumption that the sales proportions are fixed.

There are three possible approaches to preparing multi-product breakeven charts.

1 Output in $ sales and a constant product mix

2 Products in sequence

3 Output in terms of % of forecast sales and a constant product mix

P/V chart

Suppose J's sales budget is 6,000 units of M and 1,200 units of N

Revenue (6,000 × $7 + 1,200 × $15) = $60,000

Variable costs (6,000 × $3 + 1,200 × $5) = $24,000

On the chart, products are shown individually, from left to right, in order of size of decreasing C/S ratio

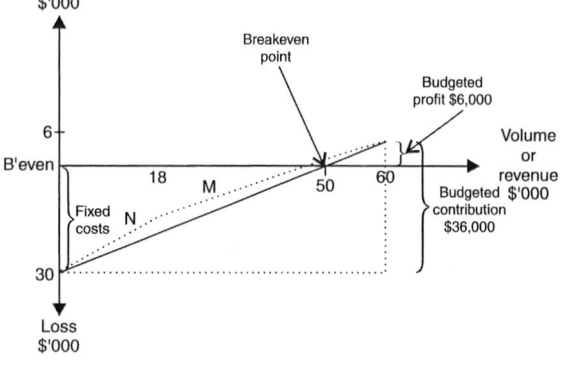

	C/S ratio	Cum sales $'000	Cum profit $'000
N	66.67%	18	*(18)
M	57.14%	60	6

* (1,200 × $15) – (12,000 × $5) – $30,000

What the multi-product P/V chart highlights

- The overall company breakeven point

- Which products should be expanded in output (the most profitable in terms of C/S ratio) and which, if any, should be discontinued

- What effect changes in selling price and sales revenue would have on breakeven point and profit

- The average profit (the solid line which joins the two ends of the dotted line) earned from the sales of the products in the mix

Advantages of CVP analysis

- Graphical representation of cost and revenue data can be more easily understood by non-financial managers.

- Highlighting the breakeven point and margin of safety gives managers an indication of the level of risk involved.

Limitations of CVP analysis

- It is assumed that fixed costs are the same in total and variable costs are the same per unit at all levels of output.

- It is assumed that sales prices will be constant at all levels of activity.

- Production and sales are assumed to be the same.

- Uncertainty in estimates of fixed costs and unit variable costs is often ignored.

6: Limiting factor analysis

Topic List

Formulating the problem

Finding the solution

Slack, surplus and shadow prices

Limiting factor analysis is a technique used to determine an optimum product mix which will maximise contribution and profit.

Linear programming is used where there is more than one resource constraint.

Example

A company makes two products, standard and deluxe.

Relevant data are as follows.

	Standard	Deluxe	Availability per month
Profit per unit	$15	$20	
Labour hours per unit	5	10	4,000
Kgs of material per unit	10	5	4,250

Step 1 Define variables

- Let x = number of standards produced each month
- Let y = number of deluxes produced each month

Step 2 Establish constraints

- Labour $5x + 10y \leq 4,000$
- Material $10x + 5y \leq 4,250$
- Non-negativity $x \geq 0, y \geq 0$

Step 3 Construct objective function

- Contribution (C) = $15x + 20y$

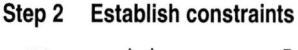

There are two methods you need to know about when finding the solution to a linear programming problem.

→ Graphical method
→ Using equations

Graphical method

Step 1   Graph the constraints

Labour $5x + 10y = 4{,}000$
if $x = 0, y = 400$
if $y = 0, x = 800$

Material $10x + 5y = 4{,}250$
if $x = 0, y = 850$
if $y = 0, x = 425$

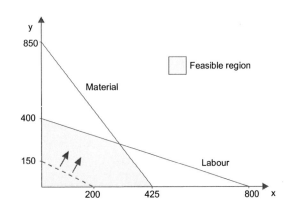

6: Limiting factor analysis

Step 2   Establish the feasible area/region

This is the area where all inequalities are satisfied (area above x axis and y axis ($x \geq 0$, $y \geq 0$), below material constraint ($\leq$) and below labour constraint ($\leq$))

Step 3   Add an iso-contribution line

Suppose C = $3,000 so that if C = 15x + 20y then if x = 0, y = 150 and if y = 0, x = 200 and (sliding your ruler across the page if necessary) find the point furthest from the origin but still in the feasible area

Step 4   Use simultaneous equations to find the x and y coordinates at the optimal solution, the intersection of the material and labour constraints (x = 300, y = 250)

Using equations

- Graph constraints and establish feasible area

- Determine all possible intersection points of constraints and axes using simultaneous equations

- Calculate profit at each intersection point to determine which is the optimal solution

Slack

Occurs when maximum availability of a resource is not used.

The resource is **not binding** at the optimal solution. Slack is associated with ≤ constraints.

Surplus

Occurs when more than a minimum requirement is used.

Surplus is associated with ≥ constraints eg a minimum production requirement.

Shadow price

It is the increase in contribution created by the availability of an extra unit of a limited resource at its original cost.

It is the maximum **premium** an organisation should be willing to pay for an extra unit of a resource.

It provides a measure of the **sensitivity** of the result.

It is only valid for a small range before the constraint becomes non-binding or different resources become critical.

6: Limiting factor analysis

Notes

7: Pricing decisions

Topic List

Pricing policy and the market

Demand

Profit maximisation

Price strategies

Pricing of an organisation's products or services is an essential part of its profitability and survival.

There are many factors influencing prices and organisations may have different price strategies.

1 Demand

- Most important factor ⟶ based on economic analysis of demand

2 Market in which the organisation operates

PERFECT COMPETITION Many buyers and sellers, one product	MONOPOLISTIC COMPETITION A large number of suppliers offer similar (not identical) products
MONOPOLY One seller who dominates many buyers	OLIGOPOLY Relatively few competitive companies dominate the market

3 Price sensitivity

- Varies amongst purchasers. If cost can be passed on – not price sensitive

4 Price perception

- How customers react to prices. If product price ↑, buy more before further rises

5 Compatibility with other products

- Eg operating systems on computers. User wants wide range of software available

6 Competitors

- Prices may move in unison (eg petrol). Alternatively, price changes may start price war

7 **Competition from substitute products**
- Eg train prices ↑, competition from coach or air travel

8 **Suppliers**
- If organisation's product price ↑, suppliers may seek price rise in supplies

9 **Inflation**
- Price changes to reflect increase in price of supplies

10 **Quality**
- Customers tend to judge quality by price

11 **Incomes**
- When household incomes rising, price not so important. When falling, important

12 **Ethics**
- Exploit short-term shortages through higher prices?

Demand is the most important factor influencing the price of a product

Price

Demand

Demand increases as prices are lowered

Price elasticity of demand (η)

A measure of the extent of change in market demand for a good, in response to a change in its price

= change in quantity demanded, as a % of demand ÷ change in price, as a % of price

Inelastic demand
- $\eta < 1$
- Steep demand curve
- Demand falls by a smaller % than % rise in price
- Pricing decision: increase prices

Elastic demand
- $\eta > 1$
- Shallow demand curve
- Demand falls by a larger % than % rise in price
- Pricing decision: decide whether change in cost will be less than change in revenue

Variables which influence demand

- The price of the good
- The price of other goods
- The size and distribution of household incomes
- Tastes and fashion
- Expectations
- Obsolescence

Demand and the individual firm

Influenced by:

- Product life cycle
- Quality
- Marketing
  - Price
  - Product
  - Place
  - Promotion

The demand equation

The equation for the demand curve is

$P = a - bQ$

P is the price

Q is the quantity demanded

a is the price at which demand = 0

b is $\dfrac{\text{change in price}}{\text{change in quantity}}$

The total cost function

Cost behaviour can be modelled using equations and linear regression analysis. A **volume-based discount** is a discount given for buying in bulk which reduces the variable cost per unit and therefore the **slope** of the cost function is less steep.

7: Pricing decisions

Determining the profit-maximising selling price/output level

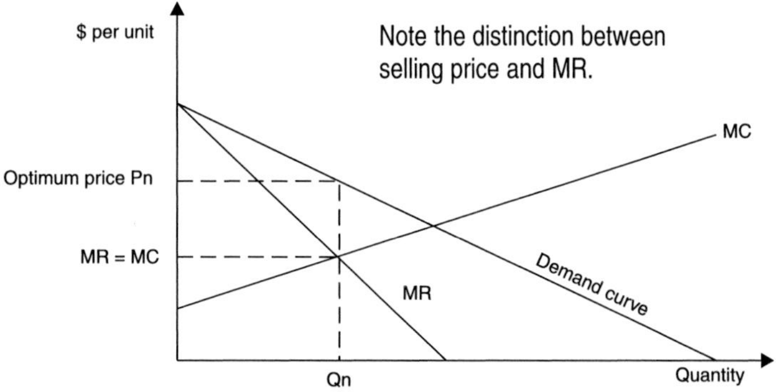

Method 1: using equations

Note the distinction between selling price and MR.

Profits are maximised when MC = MR.

Example

$MC = 320 - 0.2x$
$MR = 1{,}920 - 16.2x$

∴ Profits are maximised when
$320 - 0.2x = 1{,}920 - 16.2x$
ie when $x = 100$

You could also be provided with/asked to determine the demand curve in order to calculate the price at this profit-maximising output level.

The marginal revenue equation

$MR = a - 2bQ$

Q is the quantity demanded

a is the price at which demand = 0

b is $\dfrac{\text{change in price}}{\text{change in quantity}}$

Method 2: visual inspection of tabulation of data

1 Work out the demand curve and hence the price and total revenue (PQ) at various levels of demand.

2 Calculate total cost and hence marginal cost at each level of demand.

3 Calculate profit at each level of demand, thereby determining the price and level of demand that maximises profit.

Example

A company currently sells a product at a price of $2. Monthly sales are 60,000 units.

It has been estimated that for every $0.10 increase or decrease in the price, monthly demand will fall or rise by 1,000 units.

Costs per month are fixed costs of $60,000 and variable costs of $0.50 per unit.

What is the profit-maximising price and what would be the monthly profit at this price?

Solution

If demand equation is $P = a - bQ$

a is $2 + (60,000/1,000) \times \$0.10 = \$8$

$b = 0.10/1,000 = 0.0001$

So $P = 8 - 0.0001Q$

$MR = 8 - 0.0002Q$

$MC = 0.50$ (= marginal cost per unit)

Profit maximised where $8 - 0.0002Q = 0.50$

$Q = 37,500$

$P = 8 - (0.0001 \times 37,500) = \$4.25$ per unit

Contribution per unit = $3.75

Monthly profit = $(37,500 \times \$3.75) - \$60,000 = \$80,625$

In practice, cost is one of the most important influences on price → Full cost-plus

→ Marginal cost-plus

Full cost-plus pricing

A method of determining the sales price by calculating the full cost of the product and adding a percentage mark-up for profit.

Example

Variable cost of production
= $4 per unit
Fixed cost of production
= $3 per unit
Price is to be 40% higher than full cost

Full cost per unit = $(4 + 3) = $7

Price = $7 × $\frac{140\%}{100}$

= $9.80

Advantages

☑ Quick, simple, cheap method
☑ Ensures company covers fixed costs

Disadvantages

☒ Doesn't recognise profit-maximising combination of price and demand
☒ Budgeted output needs to be established
☒ Suitable basis for overhead absorption needed

Marginal cost-plus pricing

A method of determining the sales price by adding a profit margin onto either marginal cost of production or marginal cost of sales.

Example

Direct materials	= $15
Direct labour	= $3
Variable overhead	= $7
Price	= $40

Profit = $40 − $(15 + 3 + 7) = $15

Profit margin = $\dfrac{\$15}{\$25} \times 100\%$ = 60%

Advantages

- ☑ Simple and easy method
- ☑ Mark-up percentage can be varied
- ☑ Draws management attention to contribution

Disadvantages

- ☒ Does not ensure that attention paid to demand conditions, competitors' prices and profit maximisation
- ☒ Ignores fixed overheads – so must make sure sales price high enough to make profit

Other pricing strategies

- New products

  → Market penetration

    → low prices when product launched

  → Market skimming

    → charge high prices when product launched

- Complementary product pricing → use a 'loss leader'

- Product-line pricing → prices reflect cost proportions or demand relationships

- Volume discounting → reduction in price for large sales orders

- Relevant cost pricing → for special orders determine a minimum price

- Price discrimination → the practice of charging different prices for the same product for different groups of buyers

7: Pricing decisions

Notes

8: Short-term decisions

The overriding requirement of information needed to make decisions is relevance. Decision-making questions require a discussion of non-quantifiable factors as well as calculations to support a particular option.

Relevant costs are → Future
→ Incremental
→ Cash flows

Avoidable cost

A cost which would not be incurred if the activity to which it related did not exist.

Opportunity cost

The benefit which would have been earned but which has been given up, by choosing one option instead of another.

Relevant costs

Differential cost

The difference in the cost of alternatives.

Controllable cost

An item of expenditure which can be directly influenced by a given manager within a given time span.

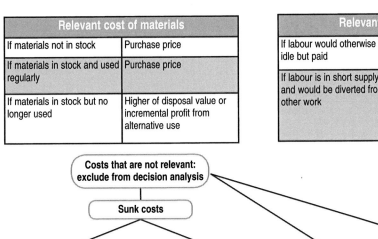

Relevant cost of materials	
If materials not in stock	Purchase price
If materials in stock and used regularly	Purchase price
If materials in stock but no longer used	Higher of disposal value or incremental profit from alternative use

Relevant cost of labour	
If labour would otherwise be idle but paid	No incremental cost. Relevant cost = 0
If labour is in short supply and would be diverted from other work	Cost of labour time plus any variable overhead plus contribution forgone by moving labour from other profitable work

Costs that are not relevant: exclude from decision analysis

Sunk costs

Costs already incurred

Costs committed by a previous decision

Non-cash expenses: depreciation

Unavoidable costs: costs that will be incurred whatever the decision, such as fixed costs

8: Short-term decisions

A make or buy problem involves a decision by an organisation about whether it should make a product/carry out an activity with its own internal resources, or whether it should pay another organisation to make the product/carry out the activity.

No scarce resource

Relevant costs are the differential costs between the two options.

With scarce resources

Where a company must subcontract work to make up a shortfall in its own production capacity, its total costs are minimised by subcontracting work which adds the least extra marginal cost per unit of scarce resource saved by subcontracting.

Example (limited labour time)

	A	B
Variable cost of making	$16	$14
Variable cost of buying	$20	$19
Extra variable cost of buying	$4	$5
Labour hours saved by buying	2	2
Extra variable cost of buying per hour saved	$2	$2.50
Priority for making in-house	2nd	1st

Outsourcing

The use of external suppliers for finished products, components or services.

Advantages	Disadvantages
☑ Superior quality and efficiency	☒ Reliability of supplier
☑ Capital is freed up	☒ Loss of control and flexibility
☑ Greater capacity and flexibility to cope with changes in demand	☒ Effect on existing workforce

Further processing decisions

A **joint product** should be processed further past the split-off point if sales revenue minus further processing costs exceeds its sales revenue at the split-off point.

The apportionment of joint processing costs is **irrelevant** to the decision.

Any short-term decision must consider qualitative factors related to the impact on employees, customers, competitors and suppliers

Shut down decisions

- Whether or not to shut down a factory/department/product line because it is making a loss or too expensive to run

- Whether closure should be permanent or temporary

1. Calculate what is earned by the process at present (perhaps in comparison with others).

2. Calculate what will be the financial consequences of closing down (selling machines, redundancy costs etc).

3. Compare the results and act accordingly.

4. Bear in mind that some fixed costs may no longer be incurred if the decision is to shut down and they are therefore relevant to the decision.

9: Risk and uncertainty

This chapter covers some of the techniques that the management accountant can use to take account of any risk or uncertainty surrounding decisions.

Topic List

Risk and uncertainty

Expected values

Decision rules

Decision trees

Value of information

Sensitivity analysis

Simulation models

Risk

Involves situations or events which may or may not occur, but whose probability of occurrence can be calculated statistically and the frequency of their occurrence predicted from past records.

Uncertainty

Involves events whose outcome **cannot** be predicted with statistical confidence.

Market research can be used to reduce uncertainty.

Attitude to risk

Risk seeker	A decision maker interested in the best outcomes no matter how small the chance that they may occur
Risk neutral	A decision maker concerned with what will be the most likely outcome
Risk averse	A decision maker who acts on the assumption that the worst outcome might occur

Expected values (EV)

Indicate what an outcome is likely to be in the long-term with repetition.

The expected value will never actually occur.

Use of EV criterion for decision-making:

1 Choose the option with highest EV of profit or lowest EV of cost.

2 Go ahead with 'yes' or 'no' decision if there is an EV of profit.

Example

If contribution could be $10,000, $20,000 or $30,000 with respective probabilities of 0.3, 0.5 and 0.2, the EV of contribution =

	$
$10,000 × 0.3	3,000
$20,000 × 0.5	10,000
$30,000 × 0.2	6,000
EV of contribution	19,000

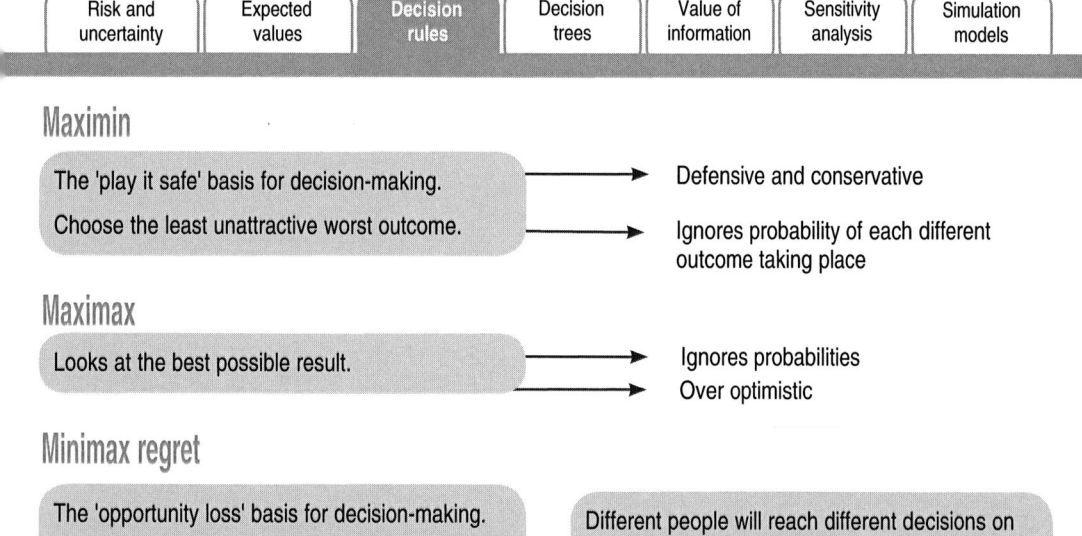

Maximin

The 'play it safe' basis for decision-making.

Choose the least unattractive worst outcome.

→ Defensive and conservative

→ Ignores probability of each different outcome taking place

Maximax

Looks at the best possible result.

→ Ignores probabilities
→ Over optimistic

Minimax regret

The 'opportunity loss' basis for decision-making.

Minimise the regret from making the wrong decision.

Different people will reach different decisions on the same problem.

Example

Profit table			
	Option A	Option B	Option C
Outcome 1	5,000	3,000	2,000
Outcome 2	4,000	6,000	4,000
Outcome 3	6,000	8,000	10,000

Regret table			
	Option A	Option B	Option C
Outcome 1	0	2,000	3,000
Outcome 2	2,000	0	2,000
Outcome 3	4,000	2,000	0

Decision: Choice of option

- **Maximin** – Choose Option A – minimum profit = $4,000

- **Maximax** – Choose Option C – maximum possible profit = $10,000

- **Minimax regret** – Choose Option B – smallest regret = $2,000

Preparation

1 Always work **chronologically** from **left to right**.

2 Start with a (labelled) **decision point.**

3 Add branches for each option/alternative.

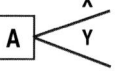

4 If the outcome of an option is 100% certain, the branch for that alternative is complete.

5 If the outcome of an option is uncertain (because there are a number of possible outcomes), add an **outcome point.**

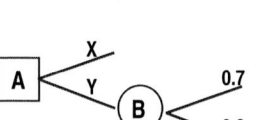

6 For each possible outcome, add a branch (with the relevant probability) to the outcome point.

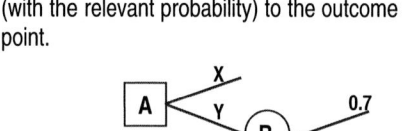

■ ■ ■ ■ ■ ■ ■ ■ ■ ■ ■ ■ ■ ■ ■ ■ ■

Evaluating the decision

Work from **right to left** and calculate the EV of revenue/cost/contribution/profit at each outcome point (**rollback analysis**).

Example

As a result of an increase in demand for a town's car parking facilities, the owners of a car park are reviewing their business operations. A decision has to be made now to select one of the following three options for the next year.

Option 1: Make no change. Annual profit is $100,000. There is little likelihood that this will provoke new competition this year.

Option 2: Raise prices by 50%. If this occurs there is a 75% chance that an entrepreneur will set up in competition this year. The Board's estimate of its annual profit in this situation would be as follows.

2A WITH a new competitor		2B WITHOUT a new competitor	
Probability	*Profit*	*Probability*	*Profit*
0.3	$150,000	0.7	$200,000
0.7	$120,000	0.3	$150,000

Option 3: Expand the car park quickly, at a cost of $50,000, keeping prices the same. The profits are then estimated to be like 2B above, except that the probabilities would be 0.6 and 0.4 respectively.

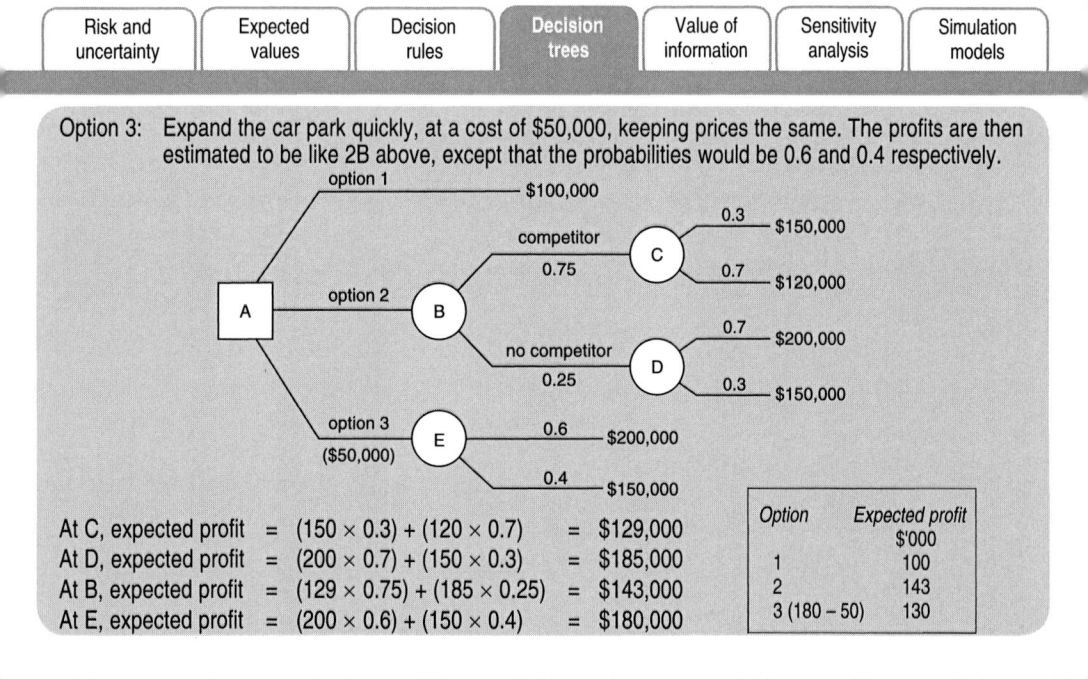

At C, expected profit = $(150 \times 0.3) + (120 \times 0.7)$ = $129,000
At D, expected profit = $(200 \times 0.7) + (150 \times 0.3)$ = $185,000
At B, expected profit = $(129 \times 0.75) + (185 \times 0.25)$ = $143,000
At E, expected profit = $(200 \times 0.6) + (150 \times 0.4)$ = $180,000

Option	Expected profit $'000
1	100
2	143
3 (180 – 50)	130

■ ■ ■ ■ ■ ■ ■ ■ ■ ■ ■ ■ ■ ■ ■

| Risk and uncertainty | Expected values | Decision rules | Decision trees | Value of information | Sensitivity analysis | Simulation models |

The value of perfect information

1. Work out the EVs of all options and see which is best.

2. See what decision would be taken with perfect information (if all the outcomes were known in advance with certainty) and calculate the EV.

3. The value of perfect information (the amount you would be willing to pay to obtain it) = EV of the action you would take with the information – EV without the information.

Alternatively a decision tree can be used.

Example

	Profit if strong demand	Profit/(loss) if weak demand
Option A	$4,000	$(1,000)
Option B	$1,500	$600
Probability	0.3	0.7

EV of A = $4,000 \times 0.3 + (1,000) \times 0.7 = \$500$
EV of B = $1,500 \times 0.3 + 600 \times 0.7 = \$870$

∴ Choose B

With perfect information, if demand is strong choose A but if demand is weak choose B.

∴ EV with perfect information = $0.3 \times 4,000 + 0.7 \times 600$
= $\$1,620$

∴ Value of perfect information = $\$(1,620 - 870)$
= $\$750$

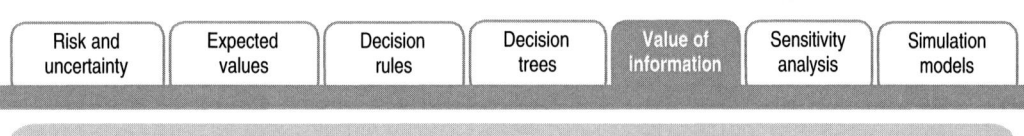

Example

X Co is trying to decide whether or not to build a shopping centre. The probability that the centre will be successful based on past experience is 0.6.

X Co could conduct market research to help with the decision.

- If the centre is going to be successful there is a 75% chance that the market research will say so
- If the centre is not going to be successful there is a 95% chance that the survey will say so

The information can be tabulated as follows.

The probabilities are as follows.

| P (research says success) | = 0.47 |
| P (research says failure) | = 0.53 |

If the survey says success

| P (success) | = 45/47 | = 0.957 |
| P (failure) | = 2/47 | = 0.043 |

If the survey says failure

| P (success) | = 15/53 | = 0.283 |
| P (failure) | = 38/53 | = 0.717 |

		Actual			
		Success	Failure	Total	
Research	Success	** 45	2	47	* given
	Failure	*** 15	38	53	** 0.75 × 60
Total		* 60	40	100	*** balancing figure

The essence of all approaches to sensitivity analysis is to carry out calculations with one set of values for the variables and then substitute other possible values for the variables to see how this effects the overall outcome.

Approach 3

Estimate by how much a variable would need to differ before a decision maker was indifferent between two options.

Approach 1 Estimate by how much a variable would need to differ from its estimated value before the decision would change.

Approach 2 Estimate whether a decision would change if a variable was X% higher than expected.

Sensitivity analysis is one form of 'what-if?' analysis

Example

Option 2 is $10,000 more expensive than option 1 and involves taking a discount of 10% from a supplier from whom you purchase $50,000 of goods (before discount) pa for 4 years. Ignore the time value of money. Discount needs to be $10,000 (difference) + $20,000 (current discount) if option 2 is as good as option 1.

$\therefore (4 \times \$50,000) \times X\% = \$30,000$

$\therefore X = 15\%$ (rate at which you are indifferent between the two options)

Simulation models

can be used to deal with decision problems involving a number of uncertain variables.

Random numbers are used to assign values to the variables.

Example

Daily demand Units	Probability	Numbers assigned
17	0.15	00-14
18	0.45	15-59
19	0.40	60-99
	1.00	

Random numbers for a simulation over three days are 761301.

Day	Random number	Demand
1	76	19
2	13	17
3	01	17

10: Budgetary systems

There are a range of budgetary systems and types which can be used. The traditional approach of incremental budgeting is not always appropriate or useful.

Topic List

Planning and control cycle

Traditional budgetary systems

Zero based budgeting (ZBB)

Other systems

Budgeting issues

The planning and control cycle

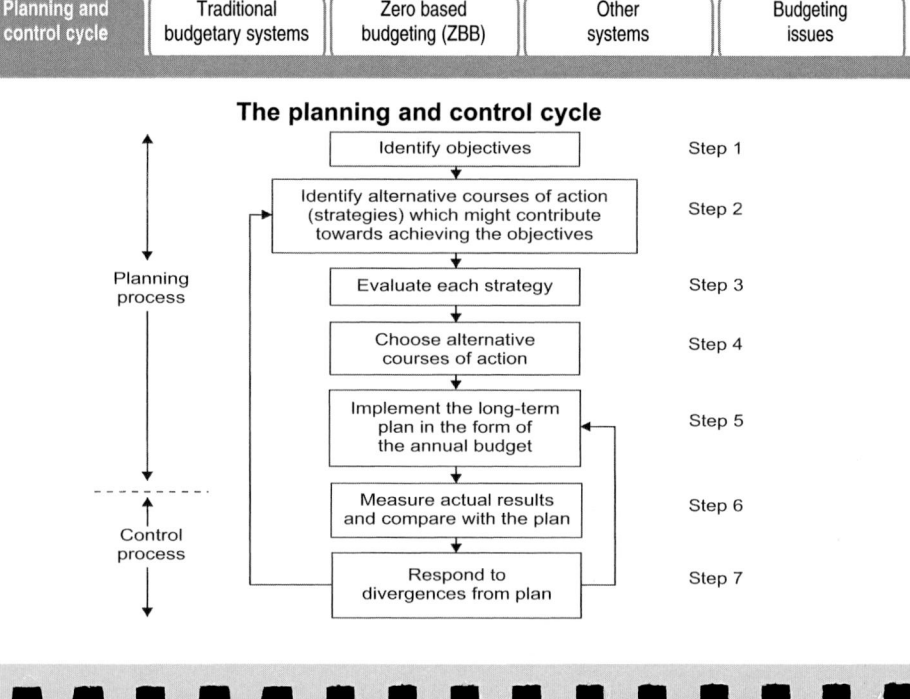

Incremental budgeting

This involves adding a certain percentage to last year's budget to allow for growth and inflation. It encourages slack and wasteful spending to creep into budgets.

Fixed budgets

These are prepared on the basis of an estimated volume of production and an estimated volume of sales. No variants of the budget are made to cover the event that actual and budgeted activity levels differ and they are not adjusted (in retrospect) to reflect actual activity levels.

Flexible budgets

These are budgets which, by recognising different cost behaviour patterns, change as activity levels change.

- At the planning stage, flexible budgets can be drawn up to show the effect of the actual volumes of output and sales differing from budgeted volumes

- At the end of a period, actual results can be compared to a flexed budget **(what results should have been at actual output and sales volumes)** as a control procedure

ZBB

This approach treats the preparation of the budget for each period as an independent planning exercise: the initial budget is zero and every item of expenditure has to be justified in its entirety to be included.

Three-step approach to ZBB

1 Define **decision packages** (description of a specific activity so that it can be evaluated and ranked).

2 Evaluate and rank packages on the basis of their benefit to the organisation.

3 Allocate resources according to the funds available and the ranking of packages.

Mutually exclusive packages   **Incremental packages**

ZBB is more useful in saving costs in administrative areas rather than in production operations or front-line services.

Advantages of ZBB	Disadvantages of ZBB
☑ Identifies and removes inefficient and/or obsolete operations	☒ Involves time and effort
☑ Provides a psychological impetus to employees to avoid wasteful expenditure	☒ Can cause suspicion when introduced
☑ Leads to a more efficient allocation of resources	☒ Costs and benefits of different alternative courses of action can be difficult to quantity
	☒ Ranking can prove problematic

Activity based budgeting (ABB)

At its simplest, ABB involves the use of costs determined using ABC in budgets. More formally, it involves defining the activities that underlie the figures in each function and using the level of activity to decide how much resource should be allocated, how well it is being managed and to explain variances from budget.

Continuous/rolling budgets

Continuous/rolling budgets are continuously updated by adding a further accounting period (month or quarter) when the earlier accounting period has expired.

Dynamic conditions making original budget inappropriate

- Organisational changes
- New technology
- Environmental considerations
- Inflation

Advantages of rolling budgets

- ☑ Reduce uncertainty
- ☑ Up to date budget always available
- ☑ Realistic budgets are better motivators

Disadvantages of rolling budgets

- ☒ Involve more time, effort and money

10: Budgetary systems

Sources of budget information

- Past data
- Sales forecasts
- Production department costing information

Allowing for uncertainty

- Flexible budgeting
- Rolling budgets
- Probabilistic budgeting
- Sensitivity analysis

Difficulties of changing budgetary practices

- Resistance by employees
- Loss of control
- Time consuming and expensive training
- Cost of implementation
- Lack of accounting information and systems in place

11: Quantitative analysis in budgeting

Topic List

Analysing fixed and variable costs

Learning curves

This chapter looks at where the figures which go into budgets come from. There are a number of quantitative techniques which are used in budgeting.

The fixed and variable elements of semi-variable costs can be determined by the **high-low method.**

Step 1   Review past records of costs

- Select period with **highest** activity level
- Select period with **lowest** activity level

Step 2   Determine

- Total cost at high activity level (TCH)
- Total cost at low activity level (TCL)
- Total units at high activity level (TUH)
- Total units at low activity level (TUL)

Step 3   Calculate variable cost per unit $= \dfrac{TCH - TCL}{TUH - TUL}$

Step 4   Determine fixed costs by substituting variable cost per unit $= TCH - (TUH \times VC \text{ per unit})$

The high-low method may give inaccurate cost estimations as it assumes costs at the extremes of activity are representative.

Theory

As **cumulative output doubles**, the **cumulative average time per unit** produced **falls** to a fixed percentage of the previous cumulative average time per unit.

Note that cumulative average time = average time per unit for all units produced so far, back to and including the first unit made.

When does learning curve theory apply?

- Product made largely by labour effort
- Brand new or relatively short-lived product
- Complex product made in small quantities for special orders

Example

Assume a 90% learning effect applies.

Cumulative output Units		Cumulative average time per unit Hours		Total time required Hours	Incremental time taken Total hours		Hours/unit
1		50.00	(× 1)	50.0			
2*	(× 90%)	45.00	(× 2)	90.0	40.0	(÷ 1)	40.0
4*	(× 90%)	40.50	(× 4)	162.0	72.0	(÷ 2)	36.0
8*	(× 90%)	36.45	(× 8)	291.6	129.6	(÷ 4)	32.4

* Output doubled each time

Formula for the learning curve

The learning effect can be shown as a learning curve.

The formula for learning curve (a) shown above is
$Y = ax^b$

where Y = cumulative average time per unit

x = the cumulative number of units

a = the time for the first unit

b = the learning coefficient or index
= log of learning rate/log of 2

This formula will be provided in the exam if it is needed.

Costs affected

- As the learning effect is a function of labour, only labour costs and other variable costs directly dependent on labour are affected

- Materials should not be affected unless early on in the learning process they are used inefficiently

- Fixed overhead expenditure should be unaffected (but some problems might be caused in an organisation that uses absorption costing)

Important note: The lower the learning curve percentage, the quicker the staff are learning.

Learning rate

When learning rate is r%, the cumulative average time per unit is r% of what it was before every time that cumulative output doubles.

Learning rate 80%		
Output units	Cumulative average time per unit (hours)	Total time to date
1	1,000	1,000
2	800	1,600
4	640	2,560
8	512	4,096

To calculate additional time for nth unit

Use the formula

Calculate cumulative average time for first $(n - 1)$ units = t_1

Calculate total time for first $(n - 1)$ units = $(n - 1) \times t_1$

Calculate cumulative average time for first n units = t_2

Calculate total time for first n units = $n \times t_2$

Calculate additional time for nth unit

= $(n \times t_2) - [(n - 1) \times t_1]$

Where learning curve theory can be used

- To calculate the marginal (incremental) cost of making extra units of a product

- To quote selling prices for a contract, where prices are calculated at a cost plus a percentage mark-up for profit

- To prepare realistic production budgets and more efficient production schedules

- To prepare realistic standard costs for cost control purposes

Limitations of learning curve theory

- Learning curve effect is not always present

- It assumes stable conditions which allow learning to take place

- It assumes a certain degree of motivation amongst employees

- Breaks between repeating production of an item must not be too long or workers will forget and learning will have to begin again

- It may be difficult to obtain enough accurate data to decide what the learning factor is

- Learning will eventually cease

12: Budgeting and standard costing

Topic List

Standard costs

Setting standards

Flexible budgets

This chapter revises standard costing and looks at how standards are set.

Flexible budgets are vital for planning and control.

Uses of standard costing

- **To act as a control device (variance analysis)**
- **To value inventories and cost production**
- To assist in setting budgets and evaluating managerial performance
- To enable the principle of 'management by exception' to be practiced
- To provide a prediction of future costs for use in decision-making situations
- To motivate staff and management by providing challenging targets
- To provide guidance on possible ways of improving efficiency

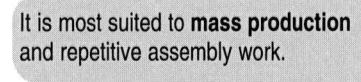

It is most suited to **mass production** and repetitive assembly work.

The responsibility for **deriving** standards should be shared between managers able to provide the necessary information about levels of expected efficiency, prices and overhead costs.

Types of performance standard

Ideal

- Perfect operating conditions
- Unfavourable motivational impact

Attainable

- Allowances made for inefficiencies and wastage
- Incentive to work harder (realistic but challenging)

Current

- Based on current working conditions
- No motivational impact

Basic

- Unaltered over a long period of time
- Unfavourable impact on performance

Ideal standards can be seen as long-term targets but are not very useful for day to day control purposes.

Current standards are useful during periods when inflation is high. They can be set on a month by month basis.

12: Budgeting and standard costing

Flexible budgets

These are budgets which, by recognising different cost behaviour patterns, change as activity levels change.

- At the planning stage, flexible budgets can be drawn up to show the effect of the actual volumes of output and sales differing from budgeted volumes
- At the end of a period, actual results can be compared to a flexed budget **(what results should have been at actual output and sales volumes)** as a control procedure

1 Decide whether costs are fixed, variable or semi-variable.

2 Split semi-variable costs into their fixed and variable components using the high-low method.

3 Flex the budget to the required activity level.

Many cost items in modern industry are **fixed costs** so the **value** of flexible budgets is dwindling.

Principle of controllability

Managers of responsibility centres should only be held accountable for costs over which they have some influence.

13: Variance analysis

Topic List

Basic variances

Operating statements

Investigating variances

Materials mix and yield variances

Sales mix and quantity variances

Variance analysis is a key technique in management accounting. You will have covered the basic variances in your earlier studies but you need to make sure you are familiar with the calculations so you can answer interpretation questions.

PM will examine the more complicated variances such as materials mix and yield.

Example to be used throughout this chapter

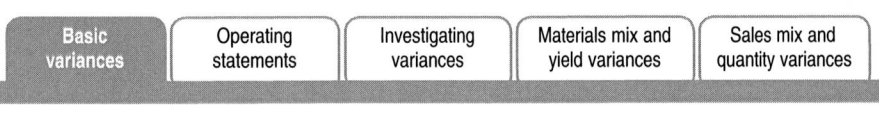

Standard cost of product A

	$
Materials (5 kg × $10 per kg)	50
Labour (4 hrs × $5 per hour)	20
Variable o/hds (4 hrs × $2 per hour)	8
Fixed o/hds (4 hrs × $6 per hour)	24
	102

Actual results

Production	1,000 units
Sales	900 units
Materials	4,850 kg, $46,075
Labour	4,200 hrs, $21,210
Variable o/hds	$9,450
Fixed o/hds	$25,000
Selling price	$140 per unit

Budgeted results

Production	1,200 units
Sales	1,000 units
Selling price	$150 per unit

■ ■ ■ ■ ■ ■ ■ ■ ■ ■ ■ ■ ■ ■ ■ ■ ■

Material total variance

The difference between what the output actually cost, and what it should have cost, in terms of material.

This can be divided into two sub-variances.

Material price variance

The difference between what the material used did cost and what it should have cost.

Material usage variance

The difference between the standard cost of the material that should have been used and the standard cost of the material that was used.

Example	
	$
1,000 units should have cost (× $50)	50,000
but did cost	46,075
Material total variance	3,925 (F)
	$
4,850 kg should have cost (× $10)	48,500
but did cost	46,075
Material price variance	2,425 (F)
1,000 units should have used	5,000 kg
but did use	4,850 kg
Variance in kg	150 kg (F)
× standard cost per kg	× $10
Material usage variance	$1,500 (F)

Labour total variance

The difference between what the output actually cost and what it should have cost, in terms of labour.

Again this can be divided into two sub-variances.

Labour rate variance

The difference between what the labour used did cost and what it should have cost.

Labour efficiency variance

The difference between the standard cost of the hours that should have been worked and that standard cost of the hours that were worked. When idle time occurs, the efficiency variance is based on hours actually worked (not hours paid for) and an **idle time variance** (hours of idle time × standard rate per hour) is calculated.

Example

	$
1,000 units should have cost (× $20)	20,000
but did cost	21,210
Labour total variance	1,210 (A)

	$
4,200 hrs should have cost (× $5)	21,000
but did cost	21,210
Labour rate variance	210 (A)

1,000 units should have used	4,000 hrs
but did use	4,200 hrs
Variance in hours	200 hrs (A)
× standard rate per hour	× $5
Labour efficiency variance	$1,000 (A)

Variable production overhead total variance

The difference between what the output should have cost and what it did cost, in terms of variable production overhead.

Variable production o/hd expenditure variance

The difference between the actual variable production overhead incurred and the amount that should have been incurred in the hours actively worked.

Variable production o/hd efficiency variance

The difference between the standard cost of the hours that should have been worked and the standard cost of the hours that were worked.

Example

	$
1,000 units should have cost (× $8)	8,000
but did cost	9,450
Variable prod o/hd total variance	1,450 (A)

	$
4,200 hrs should have cost (× $2)	8,400
but did cost	9,450
Variable prod o/hd exp'd variance	1,050 (A)

Labour efficiency variance in hrs	200 hrs (A)
× standard rate per hour	× $2
Variable prod o/hd efficiency variance	$400 (A)

The **total variance** is the difference between fixed production overhead incurred and fixed production overhead absorbed (= under- or over-absorbed fixed production overhead).

Expenditure variance

The difference between budgeted and actual fixed production overhead expenditure.

Causes of under/over-absorption

- Actual expenditure ≠ budgeted expenditure ⇒ expenditure variance
- Actual prod'n (units or hrs) ≠ budgeted prod'n ⇒ volume variance

Volume variance

The difference between actual and budgeted production units × standard absorption rate per unit.

Example

	$
Budgeted o/hd (1,200 × $24)	28,800
Actual overhead	25,000
Expenditure variance	**3,800** (F)

Example

	$
Overhead incurred	25,000
Overhead absorbed (1,000 × $24)	24,000
Under-absorbed overhead/total variance	1,000 (A)*

Example

	$
Actual prod'n at std rate (1,000 × $24)	24,000
Budgeted prod'n at std rate (1,200 × $24)	28,800
Volume variance	**4,800** (A)*

*(A) because actual output less than budgeted output

Volume efficiency variance

Shows how much of the under/over-absorption is due to efficiency of labour/plant.

The difference between the number of hours that production should have taken and the number of hours worked × standard absorption rate per hour.

This is usually the labour efficiency variance in hours and so is also similar to the variable production overhead efficiency variance.

Example

Labour efficiency variance in hrs	200 hrs (A)
× standard rate per hr	× $6
Efficiency variance	$1,200 (A)

In a marginal costing system there is no volume variance.

Volume capacity variance

Shows how much of the under/over-absorption is due to hours worked being more or less than budgeted.

The difference between budgeted hours of work and actual hours worked × standard absorption rate per hour.

Example

Budgeted hours (1,200 × 4)	4,800 hrs
Actual hours	4,200 hrs
Variance in hrs	600 hrs(A)
× std rate per hr	× $6
Capacity variance	$3,600 (A)

Selling price variance

A measure of the effect on expected profit of a different selling price to standard.

The difference between what the sales revenue should have been for the actual quantity sold, and what it was.

Example

	$
Revenue from 900 units should have been (× $150)	135,000
but was (× $140)	126,000
Selling price variance	9,000 (A)

Don't forget to value the sales volume variance at standard contribution margin if marginal costing is in use.

Sales volume variance

A measure of the effect on expected profit of a different sales volume to that budgeted.

The difference between the actual units sold and the budgeted quantity, valued at the standard profit per unit.

Example

Budgeted sales volume	1,000 units
Actual sales volume	900 units
Variance in units	100 units(A)
× std profit margin per unit (× $(150 – 102))	× $48
Sales volume variance	$4,800 (A)

| Basic variances | Operating statements | Investigating variances | Materials mix and yield variances | Sales mix and quantity variances |

Most common presentation (absorption costing)

	$	$
Budgeted profit		X
Sales variances – price	X	
– volume	X	
		X
Actual sales minus standard cost of sales		X

Cost variances	$ (F)	$ (A)	
Material price etc	X		
Fixed o/hd volume etc		X	
	X	X	X
Actual profit			X

Most common presentation (marginal costing)

	$	$
Budgeted profit		X
Budgeted fixed production overhead		X
Budgeted contribution		X
Sales variances (price and volume)		X
Actual sales minus std variable cost of sales		X
Variable cost variances		X
Actual contribution		X
Budgeted fixed production overhead	X	
Expenditure variance	X	
Actual fixed production overhead		X
Actual profit		X

Within an **ABC system** efficiency variances for longer-term variable overheads are the difference between the level of activity that should have been needed and the actual activity level, valued at the standard rate per activity.

13: Variance analysis

Reasons for variances

Material price (F) – unforeseen discounts received

              (A) – price increase, careless purchasing

Material usage (F) – material used higher quality than standard

              (A) – defective material, waste, theft

Labour rate (F) – use of less skilled (lower paid) workers

              (A) – rate increase

Idle time (always (A)) – machine breakdown, illness

Labour efficiency (F) – better quality materials

              (A) – lack of training

Overhead expenditure (F) – cost savings

              (A) – excessive use of services

Overhead volume – production greater or less than budgeted

Factors affecting the significance of variances

- Materiality
- Controllability
- Costs v benefits
- Interdependence (eg material price (F) and material usage (A))
- Type of standard used
- Variance trend

Causes of variances

- Efficient/inefficient operations
- Measurement errors
- Out of date standards
- Random/chance fluctuations

Rule of thumb method

Deciding a limit and if variance is within limit not investigated, if outside limit action is taken.

Drawbacks of method

- ☒ Limits set randomly
- ☒ Limits different for unfavourable
- ☒ Fixed percentage limits hide significant absolute losses
- ☒ Unimportant/expected fluctuations highlighted unnecessarily
- ☒ Costs/benefits of investigations not highlighted
- ☒ Past history of variances ignored

Statistical significance model

Use of historical data to calculate expected average and standard deviation. Variance investigated only if greater distance from average than normal distribution suggests is likely if process is in control.

Advantages of method

- ☑ Important costs with small variations highlighted if variances rise significantly
- ☑ Costs with normal large variations not highlighted unless variations excessive

but

How do you ascertain standard deviations of expenditure?

13: Variance analysis

If a product requires two or more raw materials, and the proportions of the materials are changeable and controllable, the materials usage variance can be split into a mix variance and a yield variance.

Materials mix variance

A measure of whether the actual mix is cheaper or more expensive than the standard and calculated as the difference between the actual total quantity used in the standard mix and the actual quantity used in the actual mix, valued at standard costs.

- Find the standard proportions of the mix
- Calculate the standard mix of the actual material used
- Find (in kg, litres etc for each input) the difference between what should have been used (as calculated above) and what was used
- Value at **standard costs**

> The mix variance in quantity is always zero.

Materials mix variance

<table>
<tr><td colspan="2" style="text-align:center">Example</td></tr>
<tr><td>Standard cost</td><td>$</td></tr>
<tr><td>Material X   2 kg at $10 per kg</td><td>20</td></tr>
<tr><td>Material Y   3 kg at $5 per kg</td><td><u>15</u></td></tr>
<tr><td></td><td><u>35</u></td></tr>
</table>

Actual usage = 280 kg of X and 320 kg of Y: total 600 kg

	Actual mix	Standard mix of actual total quantity (ratio 2:3)	Mix variance	Standard price	Mix variance
	kg	kg	kg	$ per unit	$
X	280	240	40 (A)	10	400 (A)
Y	<u>320</u>	<u>360</u>	<u>40 (F)</u>	5	<u>200 (F)</u>
	<u>600</u>	<u>600</u>	<u>0</u>		<u>200 (A)</u>

An adverse mix variance indicates a more expensive mix of materials than standard.

Materials yield variance in total

- A measure of the effect on costs of inputs yielding more or less than expected
- Calculated as the difference between the expected output from the actual input and the actual output, valued at the **standard cost** per unit of output

Example

Std input to produce 1 unit of X:

A	20 kg × $10	$200
B	30 kg × $5	$150
	50 kg	$350

In May, 13 units of X were produced from 250 kg of A and 350 kg of B.

Materials yield variance for individual materials

- Arises because there is a difference between what the inputs should have been for the output achieved and the actual inputs
- Calculated as the differences between std inputs for actual output and std mix of actual total input, valued at std costs

(250 + 350)kg should have yielded (÷ 50kg)	12X
but did yield	13X
Yield variance in units	1X (F)
× standard cost per unit of output	× $350
Yield variance in $	$350 (F)

	A	B
Std usage for actual output	260 kg	390 kg
Actual usage in std mix	240 kg	360 kg
Yield variance in kg	20 kg (F)	30 kg (F)
× std cost per kg	× $10	× $5
Yield variance in $	$200 (F)	$150 (F)

If a company sells more than one product, it is possible to analyse the overall **sales volume variance** into a sales mix variance and a sales quantity variance.

Sales mix variance

- Occurs when the proportions of the various products sold are different from those in the budget

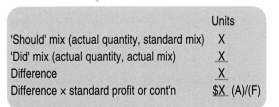

	Units
'Should' mix (actual quantity, standard mix)	X
'Did' mix (actual quantity, actual mix)	X
Difference	X
Difference × standard profit or cont'n	$X (A)/(F)

Sales quantity variance

- Shows the difference in contribution/profit because of a change in sales volume from the budgeted volume of sales

	Units
Actual sales (standard mix)	X
Standard sales (standard mix)	X
Difference	X
Difference × standard profit or cont'n	$X (A)/(F)

Example

Budgeted sales	Units	Std profit per unit	Budgeted profit
Product		$	$
A	500	8	4,000
B	1,000	5	5,000
	1,500		9,000

Weighted average standard profit per unit = $9,000/1,500 = $6

Actual sales = 700 units of A and 740 units of B

Sales quantity variance

	Units
Budgeted total sales	1,500
Actual total sales (700 + 740)	1,440
Sales quantity variance (units)	60 (A)
Weighted avge std profit	$6
Sales quantity variance in $	$360 (A)

	Actual sales mix	Standard mix of actual total quantity (ratio 1:2)	Mix variance	Standard price	Mix variance
	units	units	units	$ per unit	$
A	700	480	220 (F)	8	1,760 (A)
B	740	960	220 (A)	5	1,100 (F)
	1,440	1,440	0		660 (F)

14: Planning and operational variances

When a standard cost is revised during a budget period, variances can be analysed into planning variances (for which operational managers are not responsible) and operational variances (which are the responsibility of an operational manager).

Planning variances

Arise because of inaccurate planning/faulty standards and so not controllable by operational managers but by senior management.

Calculated by comparing an original standard with a revised standard.

Operational variances

Caused by adverse/favourable operational performance.

Calculated by comparing actual results with a realistic, revised standard/budget.

Disadvantages

- ☒ Difficulty in determining realistic standards
- ☒ Danger of managers attempting to explain all variances as planning errors
- ☒ Time-consuming preparation
- ☒ Do not provide an overall picture of the total variance

Advantages

- ☑ Highlight controllable and uncontrollable variances
- ☑ Increase both managers' acceptance of the use of variances for performance measurement and managers' motivation
- ☑ Improve planning and standard-setting processes as standards are more accurate, relevant and appropriate
- ☑ Operational variances provide a fairer reflection of actual performance

Revised budget

A **revised budget** can be calculated using revised standards so that only **operational variances** are highlighted when actual results are compared to the revised budget.

Total planning and operational variances

Example

The standard material cost of a product is $3 (3 kg × $1). Actual material costs were $250,000 when 70,000 units were made and 200,000 kg of material were used. With the benefit of hindsight, management realises that a more realistic standard material cost for current conditions would be $4.20 (3.5 kg × $1.20).

	$
Revised standard cost	
(70,000 × $4.20)	294,000
Original standard cost	
(70,000 × $3)	210,000
Total planning variance	84,000 (A)

	$
70,000 units should have cost	
(using revised std of $4.20)	294,000
but did cost	250,000
Total operational variance	44,000 (F)

Example

Original sales budget = 5,000 units per month, based on expected market share of 20%

Standard profit per unit = $8

In retrospect, market size re-estimated at 35,000 units per month

So in retrospect revised budget sales should have been 7,000 units = 20% of market

Actual sales = 7,200 units

Market size variance (= sales volume planning variance)

	Units
Original sales budget	5,000
Revised sales budget	7,000
Market size variance in units	2,000 (F)
Standard profit per unit	$8
Market size variance in $ profit	$16,000 (F)

Market share variance (= sales volume operational variance)

	Units
Expected sales (revised budget)	7,000
Actual sales	7,200
Market share variance in units	200 (F)
Standard profit per unit	$8
Market share variance in $ profit	$1,600 (F)

Example

Original standard material cost: 3 kg at $6 per kg = $18
Revised standard cost: 4 kg at $5 per kg = $20
Actual production = 2,000 units. They used 8,300 kg, costing $40,800.

Material price planning variance

	$
Original standard price	6
Revised standard price	5
Price planning variance	1 (F)
Quantity used (kg)	8,300
Price planning variance	$8,300 (F)

Material price operational variance

	$
8,300 kg should cost (× $5)	41,500
They did cost	40,800
Price operational variance	700 (F)

Material usage planning variance		Material usage operational variance	
For 2,000 units output:	kg		kg
Original standard usage	6,000	2,000 units should use (× 4)	8,000
Revised standard usage	8,000	They did use	8,300
Usage planning variance in kg	2,000 (A)	Usage variance in kg	300 (A)
Original standard price per kg	$6	**Original** standard price per kg	$6
Usage planning variance in $	$12,000 (A)	Usage operational variance	$1,800 (A)

Example

Original standard direct labour cost: 2 hours at $10 per hour = $20

Revised standard cost: 1.5 hours at $16 per hour = $24

Actual production = 3,000 units. They took 4,100 hours to make: labour cost $64,000

Labour rate planning variance

	$ per hour
Original standard rate	10
Revised standard rate	16
Rate planning variance	6 (A)
Actual hours	4,100
Rate planning variance	$24,600 (A)

Labour rate operational variance

	$
4,100 hours should cost (× $16)	65,600
They did cost	64,000
Price operational variance	1,600 (F)

Labour efficiency planning variance		Labour efficiency operational variance	
For 3,000 units output:	hours		hours
Original standard time (× 2)	6,000	3,000 units should take (× 1.5)	4,500
Revised standard time (× 1.5)	4,500	They did take	4,100
Efficiency planning var in hrs	1,500 (F)	Efficiency variance in hours	400 (F)
Original standard rate per hr	$10	**Original** standard rate per hr	$10
Efficiency planning var in $	$15,000 (F)	Efficiency operational variance	$4,000 (F)

15: Performance analysis and behavioural aspects

Topic List

Using variance analysis

Behavioural implications

TQM, JIT and standard costs

Changing environment

Performance targets should provide a motivation, and performance reporting should act as a guide to control action. However behavioural issues can affect both budgeting and control activities. Performance reporting with standard costs is now inappropriate for some modern manufacturing environments.

Responsibility for variances	
Planning variances	Planning managers
Sales price	Sales management
Sales volume	Sales management; but production management if poor sales are attributable to production problems
Material price	Purchasing manager (usually)
Material usage and labour efficiency	Production manager
Labour rate	Manager responsible for negotiating pay rate. Production manager for excess hiring and overtime premiums

Variances are historical performance measures, but they should be a guide to controlling action and improving performance **in the future**.

The level of difficulty in the budget affects reported variances:

- **Ideal standard** – variances always adverse
- **Target standard** – variances will often be adverse
- **Current standard** – no motivation to improve

Objectives of a budgetary planning and control system

- Ensure the organisation's objectives are achieved
- Compel planning
- Communicate ideas and plans
- Co-ordinate activities
- Provide a framework for responsibility accounting
- Establish a system of control
- Motivate employees to improve their performance

Negative effects of budgets include

- **At the planning stage**
  - Managers may fail to co-ordinate plans with those of other budget centres.
  - They may build slack into expenditure estimates.
- **When putting plans into action**
  - Minimal co-operation and communication between managers.
  - Managers might try to achieve targets but not beat them.
- **Using control information**
  - Resentment, managers seeing the information as part of a system of trying to find fault with their work.
  - Scepticism of the value of information if it is inaccurate, too late or not understood.

Budgets as targets

Can budgets, as targets, motivate managers to achieve a high level of performance?

- **Ideal standards** are demotivating because adverse efficiency variances are always reported
- **Low standards** are demotivating because there is no sense of achievement in attainment, no impetus to try harder
- **Normal levels** of attainment can encourage **budgetary slack**

To ensure managers are properly motivated, two budgets can be used:

- One for planning and decision-making, based on reasonable expectations **(expectations budget)**
- One for motivational purposes, with more difficult targets **(aspirations budget)**

Budgetary slack

The difference between the minimum necessary costs and the costs built into the budget or actually incurred.

→ Managers might deliberately overestimate costs and underestimate sales so that they will not be blamed for overspending and poor results.

| Using variance analysis | Behavioural implications | TQM, JIT and standard costs | Changing environment |

Total Quality Management (TQM)

- Aspects of TQM
- Kaizen = continuous improvement. Performance should improve continually. No such thing as an established 'standard performance'
- Eliminate all waste
- Quality matters more than quantity

Just-in-Time (JIT) production

- Do not produce output unless there is a sales order
- Do not purchase materials until needed for production
- Idle resources are inevitable and acceptable, although management should try to minimise this

Standard costs are inconsistent with
TQM and JIT principles

Standard costs

Variances are improved by working at full capacity

Favourable efficiency variances to produce more output = good

Idle time creates an adverse variance

Quantity matters: quality is ignored

Standard costs allow for waste and include 'normal loss'

15: Performance analysis and behavioural aspects

Problems with standard costing

- Concentrates on a narrow range of costs
- Too much emphasis on direct labour costs and other short-term variable costs
- Relies on repetitive operation and homogenous output
- Business environment is increasingly dynamic and unstable
- Information produced is not sufficient timely

Why is it still used?

- Organisations still need to plan and quantify budgets
- Cost and mix changes from plan still relevant
- Use standards as a starting point in cost construction for a new product
- Used for product pricing
- Trends can be monitored over time
- Accounting valuations

Participation

Budget-setting styles

- Imposed (from the top down)
- Participative (from the bottom up)
- Negotiated

In practice final budgets are likely to lie between what top management would really like and what junior managers believe is feasible.

Advantages of participative approach include

☑ More realistic budgets

☑ Co-ordination, morale and motivation improved

☑ Increased management commitment to objectives

Disadvantages of participative approach include ➤ If employees feel they do not have the necessary skills, think that the budget will be used against them or complain that are too busy, participation could be an added pressure rather than an opportunity.

☒ More time-consuming

☒ Budgetary slack may be introduced

☒ Does not suit some employees

15: Performance analysis and behavioural aspects

16: Performance management in private sector organisations

Topic List

Performance measurement

Balanced scorecard

Building Block model

Performance measurement aims to establish how well something or someone is doing in relation to a planned activity. It is a vital part of the control process and can be done using financial and non-financial performance indicators. Remember that different performance measures are appropriate for different organisations.

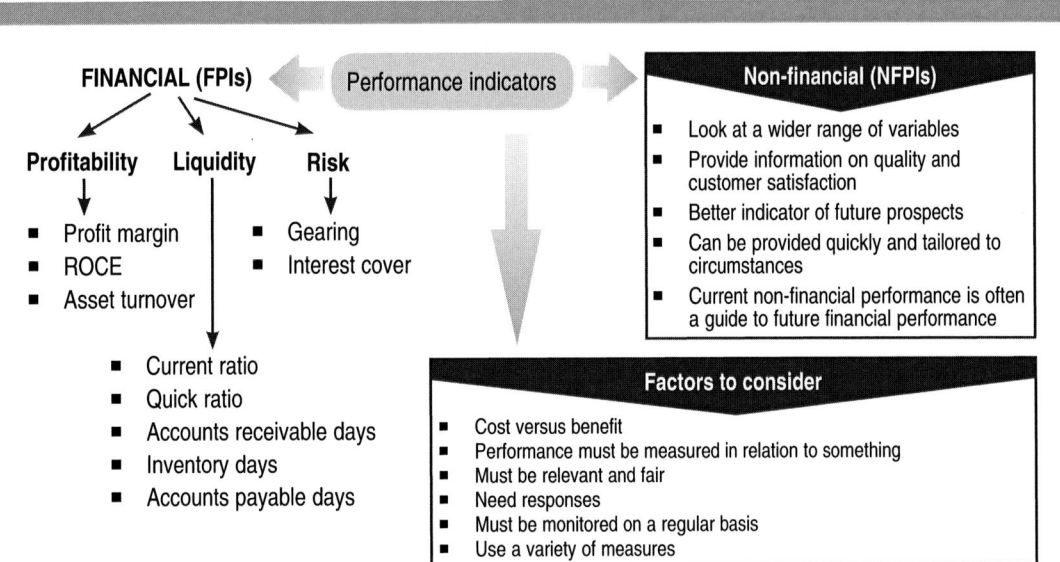

FINANCIAL (FPIs) ← Performance indicators → **Non-financial (NFPIs)**

Profitability   **Liquidity**   **Risk**

- Profit margin
- ROCE
- Asset turnover

- Gearing
- Interest cover

- Current ratio
- Quick ratio
- Accounts receivable days
- Inventory days
- Accounts payable days

Non-financial (NFPIs)

- Look at a wider range of variables
- Provide information on quality and customer satisfaction
- Better indicator of future prospects
- Can be provided quickly and tailored to circumstances
- Current non-financial performance is often a guide to future financial performance

Factors to consider

- Cost versus benefit
- Performance must be measured in relation to something
- Must be relevant and fair
- Need responses
- Must be monitored on a regular basis
- Use a variety of measures

Short-termism

Where there is a bias towards short-term rather than long-term performance.

Examples	Methods to encourage a long-term view
■ Protecting short-term cash flow and profit by abandoning capital expenditure	■ Make short-term targets realistic
■ Saving costs by cutting R&D	■ Provide sufficient management information
■ Reducing quality control, customer service or training to cut costs	■ Link managers' rewards to share price
	■ Set quality based and multiple targets

With a balanced scorecard, targets are set and performance is measured for four different perspectives of performance.

Perspective	Question	Explanation
Customer	What do existing and new customers value from us?	Gives rise to targets that matter to customers: cost, quality, delivery, inspection, handling and so on
Internal	What processes must we excel at to achieve our financial and customer objectives?	Aims to improve internal processes and decision-making
Innovation and learning	Can we continue to improve and create future value?	Considers the business's capacity to maintain its competitive position through the acquisition of new skills and the development of new products
Financial	How do we create value for our shareholders?	Covers traditional measures such as growth, profitability and shareholder value but set through talking to the shareholder or shareholders direct

The Building Block model attempts to overcome the problems associated with performance measurement of service businesses. (Fitzgerald and Moon, 1996)

Building Blocks

Service characteristics	Standards	Rewards	Dimensions
■ Intangibility ■ Inseparability ■ Perishability ■ Variability ■ No transfer of ownership	■ Individuals need a sense of ownership of targets ■ Achievable ■ Equity: standards should be fair	■ Clearly understood ■ Motivate individuals ■ Controllability: managers should be able to control their areas of responsibility	■ Competitive performance ■ Financial performance ■ Quality of service ■ Flexibility ■ Resource utilisation ■ Innovation

16: Performance management in private sector organisations

Notes

17: Divisional performance and transfer pricing

Topic List

Divisionalisation

Performance measures

Transfer pricing

When organisations have a divisional structure, divisional performance measures will be required and transfer pricing may be used.

There are two common ways of structuring organisations. → Functionally
                                                          → Divisionally

In general, a divisional structure will lead to decentralisation of the decision-making process.

Advantages of divisionalisation	Disadvantages of divisionalisation

☑ It can improve the decision-making process in two ways
   ■ Quality
   ■ Speed
☑ The authority to act to improve performance should motivate divisional managers
☑ Top management are freed from detailed involvement in day to day operations and can devote more time to strategic planning
☑ Divisions provide valuable training grounds for future members of top management
	☒ **Dysfunctional decision-making** (a balance has to be kept between decentralisation of authority to provide incentives and motivation, and retaining centralised authority to ensure **goal congruence**)
	☒ Increase in costs of activities common to all divisions
	☒ Loss of control by top management

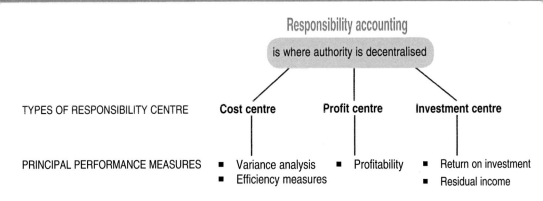

Return on investment (ROI) = $\dfrac{\text{Profit before interest}}{\text{Capital employed}} \times 100\%$

Residual income = Profit − Notional interest cost

RI and ROI

- RI will increase when investments earning above the cost of capital are undertaken
- Under ROI a marginally profitable investment is less likely to be undertaken
- RI is more flexible as different costs of capital can be used to reflect different risk
- RI does not facilitate comparisons between investment centres
- RI does not relate the size of a centre's income to the size of the investment

Aims

- Promote divisional autonomy
- Equitable divisional performance measurement
- Overall corporate profit maximisation

Transfer price

The price at which goods and services are transferred from one division to another.

minimum

Marginal cost plus opportunity cost of item transferred

Opportunity cost is the maximum contribution foregone by transferring internally

maximum

Lowest external market price minus internal cost saving on packaging and delivery

Disadvantages

- [X] Market price may be temporary
- [X] Disincentive to use up spare capacity
- [X] No market price available
- [X] Imperfect external market

17: Divisional performance and transfer pricing

Transfer prices based on cost

If there is **no external market**, the transfer price has to be based on cost.

1	**Standard or actual?**	The use of standard costs is fairer because if actual costs are used the transferring division has no incentive to control its costs – it can pass on its inefficiencies to the receiving division.
2	**Variable cost?**	The transferring division does not cover its fixed costs (although this problem can be overcome by central decisions or by some form of **dual pricing** or **two-part charging** system).
3	**Full cost?**	The transferring division makes no profit.
4	**Full cost plus?**	What margin will all parties perceive as fair?

Optimal transfer price

Reflects opportunity costs and where there is a perfect external market this will be the market price. If not, the ideal transfer price will be found by negotiation and careful analysis.

18: Further aspects of performance management

Topic List

Not-for-profit organisations

External considerations

Behaviour aspects

Not-for-profit organisations and the public sector have non-quantifiable and multiple objectives which causes problems in performance measurement.

Organisations must also consider external influences on performance.

Not-for-profit organisations

They have a range of multiple objectives which are difficult to define.

Value for money

- **Efficiency:** Relationship between inputs and outputs (getting out as much as possible for what goes in)

- **Effectiveness:** Relationship between outputs and objectives (getting done what was supposed to be done)

- **Economy:** Obtaining the right quality and quantity of inputs at lowest cost (being frugal)

Problem with performance measurement

- Multiple objectives
- Measuring outputs
- Lack of profit measure
- Nature of service provided
- Financial constraints
- Political, social and legal considerations

Solutions

- Judge performance in terms of inputs
- Use experts' subjective judgement
- Use benchmarking
- Use unit cost quantitative measures

Performance measurement needs to allow for external considerations.

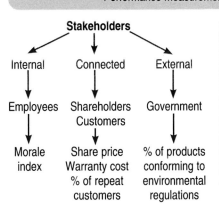

Stakeholders

Internal → Employees → Morale index

Connected → Shareholders Customers → Share price Warranty cost % of repeat customers

External → Government → % of products conforming to environmental regulations

Market conditions

- Economic growth
- Local economic trends
- Inflation
- Interest rates
- Exchange rates
- Government fiscal policy
- Government spending

Competitors

- Pricing strategies
- Information on competitors' prices and cost structures
- React quickly to changing market conditions

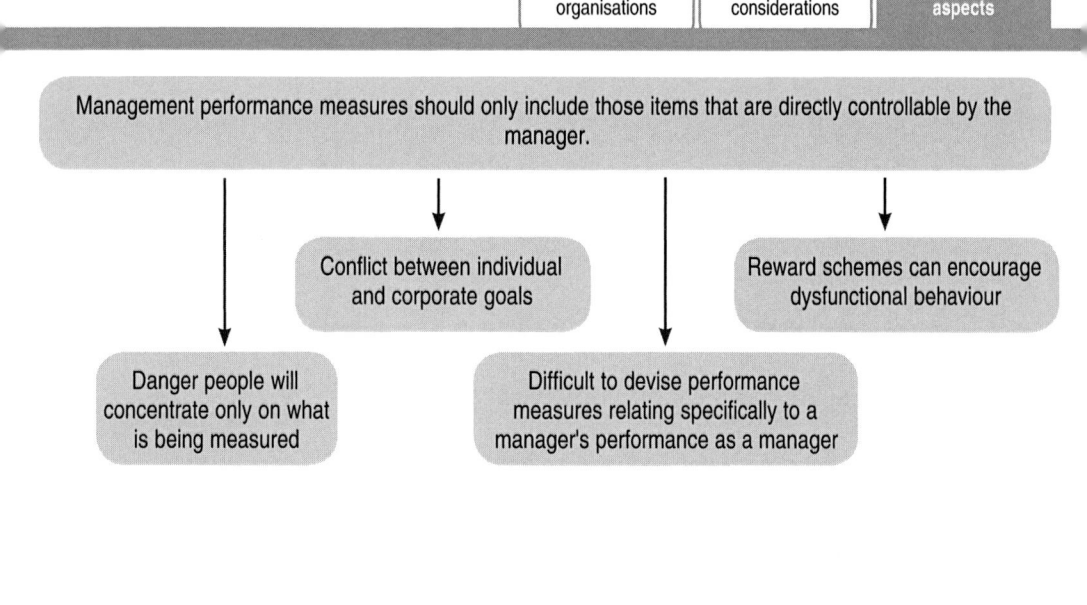

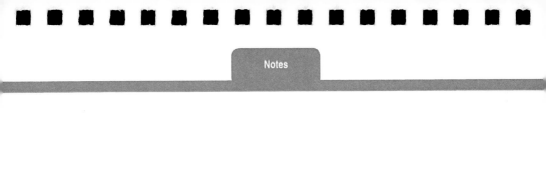

Notes

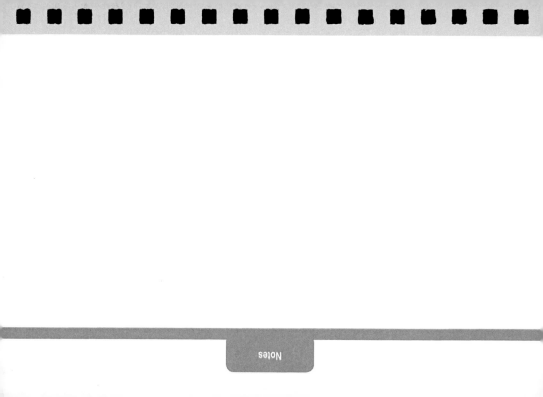

Notes

Notes

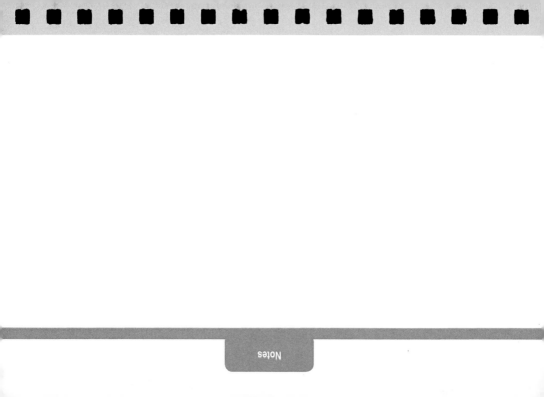

Notes

Notes

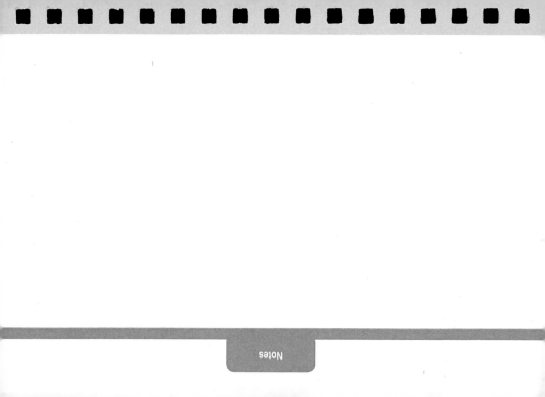

Notes